# WHY DON'T JELLYFISH HAVE BRAINS?

## AND OTHER ODD INVERTEBRATE ADAPTATIONS

BY CAITIE McANENEY

**Gareth Stevens**
PUBLISHING

Please visit our website, www.garethstevens.com. For a free color catalog of all our high-quality books, call toll free 1-800-542-2595 or fax 1-877-542-2596.

**Library of Congress Cataloging-in-Publication Data**

Names: McAneney, Caitie, author.
Title: Why don't jellyfish have brains? : and other odd invertebrate
  adaptations / Caitie McAneney.
Description: New York : Gareth Stevens Publishing, [2019] | Series: Odd
  adaptations | Includes index.
Identifiers: LCCN 2017058107| ISBN 9781538220399 (library bound) | ISBN
  9781538220412 (paperback) | ISBN 9781538220429 (6 pack)
Subjects: LCSH: Jellyfishes–Adaptation–Juvenile literature. |
  Invertebrates–Adaptation–Juvenile literature. | Adaptation
  (Biology)–Juvenile literature.
Classification: LCC QL377.S4 M33 2019 | DDC 593.5/3–dc23
LC record available at https://lccn.loc.gov/2017058107

First Edition

Published in 2019 by
**Gareth Stevens Publishing**
111 East 14th Street, Suite 349
New York, NY 10003

Copyright © 2019 Gareth Stevens Publishing

Designer: Sarah Liddell
Editor: Therese Shea

Photo credits: Cover, p. 1 Rada Photos/Shutterstock.com; background used throughout Captblack76/Shutterstock.com; p. 4 Butterfly Hunter/Shutterstock.com; p. 5 KarSol/Shutterstock.com; p. 6 V Devolder/Shutterstock.com; p. 7 Karen Adamczewski/Shutterstock.com; p. 9 feathercollector/Shutterstock.com; p. 10 Gondwananet/Wikimedia Commons; p. 11 (box jellyfish) Chris Troch/Shutterstock.com; p. 11 (blue-ringed octopus) YUSRAN ABDUL RAHMAN/Shutterstock.com; p. 11 (deathstalker scorpion) Zigi/Wikimedia Commons; p. 11 (Brazilian wandering spider) Nashepard/Shutterstock.com; p. 11 (marbled cone snail) Bricktop/Wikimedia Commons; p. 12 Mike Hewitt - FIFA/Contributor/FIFA/Getty Images; p. 13 Handout/Handout/Getty Images News/Getty Images; p. 14 Glass and Nature/Shutterstock.com; p. 15 pictoplay/Shutterstock.com; p. 16 SIMON SHIM/Shutterstock.com; p. 17 Cathy Keifer/Shutterstock.com; p. 18 Marek R. Swadzba/Shutterstock.com; p. 19 Kseniya Lanzarote/Shutterstock.com; p. 21 3Dstock/Shutterstock.com; p. 22 Natalia Siiatovskaia/Shutterstock.com; p. 23 Wolfgang Poelzer/WaterFrame/Getty Images; p. 24 Damsea/Shutterstock.com; p. 25 zaferkizilkaya/Shutterstock.com; p. 26 Josve05a/Wikimedia Commons; p. 27 Pong Wira/Shutterstock.com; p. 28 daoh/Shutterstock.com; p. 29 Bill45/Shutterstock.com.

Printed in the United States of America

CPSIA compliance information: Batch #CS18GS: For further information contact Gareth Stevens, New York, New York at 1-800-542-2595.

# CONTENTS

Words in the glossary appear in **bold** type the first time they are used in the text.

# AMAZING ADAPTATIONS

The animal kingdom is full of amazing adaptations. **LIVING THINGS ADAPT IN ORDER TO SURVIVE IN THEIR HABITATS.** Adaptations start out as **mutations**. If a mutation is helpful, it's passed down from parents to their young. Over time, this mutation—even if it seems odd—becomes normal.

Some adaptations are physical, or body, characteristics. These are called structural adaptations. An example is the hard shell of a crab, which keeps it safe from predators. Other adaptations have to do with behavior. Monarch butterflies' journey south to Mexico each year is a behavioral adaptation. They travel thousands of miles to live in warm weather through winter!

**MONARCH BUTTERFLY**

## ADAPTATIONS AID

Adaptations serve different purposes. Some help predators hunt prey. Others help prey stay safe from predators. Many adaptations deal with a living thing's environment, or surroundings. Animals in the Arctic may have white fur to blend in with snow. Animals living in the deep sea have special senses for living in the dark.

A COMMON ADAPTATION IS CAMOUFLAGE, OR A SHAPE, COLOR, OR BEHAVIOR THAT HELPS ANIMALS BLEND IN WITH THEIR ENVIRONMENT. BUGS CALLED WALKING STICKS ARE SHAPED AND COLORED LIKE TWIGS ON THE FOREST FLOOR!

# INCREDIBLE INVERTEBRATES

Invertebrates are animals without a bony skeleton or backbone. They're the most successful of all animals, which means there are a lot of them! **ABOUT 97 PERCENT OF ALL ANIMALS ARE INVERTEBRATES—AND MOST OF THESE ARE INSECTS.** Other invertebrates are corals, crabs, spiders, worms, and octopuses. Sea sponges and jellyfish are also invertebrates. Invertebrates range in size from **microscopic** to giant.

So many different kinds of invertebrates means many kinds of adaptations. It's not hard to find some odd ones. **WEIRD INVERTEBRATE ADAPTATIONS INCLUDE KILLER POISON, THE ABILITY TO LIVE WITHOUT A BRAIN, AND EVEN MIND CONTROL!**

## THE FIRST CREATURES ON EARTH

Scientists study ancient creatures through their fossils, and they make discoveries every day. For a time, scientists thought that the first creature on Earth was the ocean-drifting comb jellyfish. Now they believe sea creatures called sponges were the first. Both these invertebrates still exist today, millions of years later.

SEA SPONGE

SCIENTISTS THINK
THERE MIGHT BE MORE THAN
30 MILLION SPECIES, OR
KINDS, OF INVERTEBRATES ON
EARTH! SO FAR, ONLY ABOUT
1.25 MILLION SPECIES HAVE
BEEN DISCOVERED.

# NOT THAT BRAINY

Jellyfish have a misleading name. They're not fish. They don't have bones or a heart like a fish does. They also lack a head, eyes, ears, nose, and legs. **AND EVEN THOUGH THEY LOOK A BIT LIKE A FLOATING BRAIN WITH TENTACLES, THEY DON'T HAVE A BRAIN!**

So, what *are* jellyfish? They're invertebrates with a jellylike body. They drift along using water currents or swim by opening and closing their bell-shaped body. Most have long tentacles that can catch food or sting predators. While they lack a brain, they have a basic **nervous system** called a nerve net. Their bodies can "feel" things and sense light, too.

## GLOW-IN-THE-DARK JELLYFISH

**ABOUT HALF OF JELLYFISH SPECIES CAN PRODUCE LIGHT. THIS ADAPTATION IS CALLED BIOLUMINESCENCE.** Many sea creatures can produce light, especially those living in dark, deep waters. Jellyfish use this ability to defend themselves against predators. They flash light to scare enemies. They may even release, or let go of, a glowing tentacle to confuse predators!

YOU CAN SEE THE
BIOLUMINESCENCE OF
THIS JELLYFISH, CALLED THE
JAPANESE SEA NETTLE.

# DEATH BY POISON

Jellyfish don't have to have brains to be deadly. **ALL JELLYFISH ARE VENOMOUS. THAT MEANS THEY HAVE THE ABILITY TO HARM LIVING THINGS WITH VENOM, OR POISON, THEIR BODY PRODUCES.** This adaptation is a defense against predators. Jellyfish have stingers on their tentacles and sometimes their bell to deliver the venom. The venom also allows jellyfish to kill or **paralyze** prey.

Some jellyfish can seriously hurt or kill humans. In fact, a few are the most venomous creatures on Earth! Irukandji jellyfish are tiny, see-through creatures that live in waters around Australia. Swimmers there have died after being stung by this species.

**IRUKANDJI JELLYFISH**

## BOX JELLYFISH

Box jellyfish have a square-shaped bell, which is where their name comes from. They can grow to be 10 feet (3 m) long. **THEIR PAINFUL VENOM ATTACKS A VICTIM'S SKIN CELLS, NERVOUS SYSTEM, AND HEART.** The most dangerous box jellyfish live in the warm waters of the Indian and Pacific Oceans.

# KILLER INVERTEBRATES

**BLUE-RINGED OCTOPUS**

**BRAZILIAN WANDERING SPIDER**

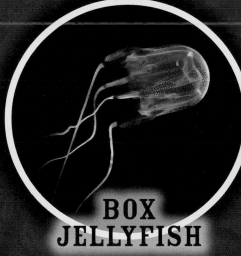

**BOX JELLYFISH**

**MARBLED CONE SNAIL**

**DEATHSTALKER SCORPION**

**VENOM IS AN ADAPTATION THAT MAKES UP FOR THESE DEADLY INVERTEBRATES' SMALL SIZE!**

# MONSTERS OF THE DEEP

Imagine a creature with eyes as big as soccer balls. Together, its body and arms are taller than a house. This monster-sized creature is the colossal squid. It's an invertebrate that has inspired sea monster stories for hundreds of years. **SCIENTISTS THINK ADULT COLOSSAL SQUIDS GROW TO BE 60 FEET (18 M) LONG!**

The colossal squid's size is enough to keep most predators away. However, it also has plenty of other adaptations to survive the deep waters near Antarctica. The squid's huge eyes help it see in the dark and watch for both prey and predators. In fact, its eyes have light organs that act like headlights!

## SUPERSIZED SPIDER CRAB

If you have a fear of spiders or crabs, the Japanese spider crab might be your worst nightmare. This invertebrate is the largest of all crabs. **FROM TIP TO TIP, ITS LEGS CAN MEASURE NEARLY 15 FEET (4.6 M)!** Spider crab bodies are protected with a hard outer covering, called an exoskeleton, which blends in with the ocean floor.

YOU PROBABLY WON'T RUN INTO A COLOSSAL SQUID. THE ONES PEOPLE USUALLY SEE ARE DEAD BY THE TIME THEY REACH THE WATER'S SURFACE.

# MIND CONTROL

Some invertebrates are parasites, or animals that harm others for their own benefit. The jewel wasp, also called the emerald cockroach wasp, grows to be less than 1 inch (2.5 cm) long. However, it can take on much larger insects using killer adaptations.

A jewel wasp uses its senses of smell and sight to find its victim—a cockroach. It stings and paralyzes the cockroach. **THEN, THE WASP INJECTS VENOM INTO THE COCKROACH'S BRAIN TO MAKE IT A "ZOMBIE."** The wasp leads the zombie cockroach to a den, where it lays an egg on the cockroach's leg. The egg hatches, and the larva eats the cockroach's insides!

**JEWEL WASPS USE THE ADAPTATION OF MIND CONTROL SO THEIR YOUNG CAN SURVIVE.**

## PESKY PARASITES

Most invertebrate parasites are smaller than their "hosts," but they use effective adaptations to gain control over them. Body parts such as claws or hooks attach to a host's body, while sucking mouthparts help the parasites eat. Common parasites that bother humans include lice, fleas, mosquitoes, and tapeworms.

**TAPEWORM**

# DISGUISED AS DROPPINGS

Camouflage is a useful adaptation seen across the animal kingdom. Hickory horned devil caterpillars turn into regal moths. However, they start their lives as small blackish larvae. They have few defenses from hungry predators, such as birds. So, they eat at night and sleep during the day curled into a "J" shape. **THEY LOOK LIKE BIRD POOP, SO BIRDS OVERLOOK THEM!**

The larvae **molt** four times until they're about 6 inches (15 cm) long and as thick as a hot dog. By this time, hickory horned devil caterpillars are green or orange and have spiky horns on their head—another adaptation to scare away predators.

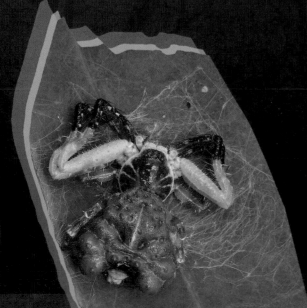

## BIRD-DUNG CRAB SPIDER

It's hard to find a creature on Earth that's less appealing than the bird-dung crab spider. These spiders gather their legs in and sit still for long periods of time. Like hickory horned devil larvae, their coloring and shape make them look like bird poop. **SOME EVEN** *SMELL LIKE POOP!*

WITH EACH MOLT, THE HICKORY HORNED DEVIL CATERPILLAR CHANGES COLORS, FROM YELLOW TO BROWN TO ORANGE TO FINALLY GREEN.

# A BUG WITH NO BITE

What happens when you see a yellow-and-black striped bug flying towards you? Chances are, you run! In nature, yellow-and-black coloring is a common warning to avoid stinging insects, such as wasps, hornets, and bees.

**HOVERFLIES ARE COMPLETELY HARMLESS. HOWEVER, THEY MIMIC, OR COPY, STINGING ANIMALS WITH THEIR YELLOW-AND-BLACK COLORING.** They may gather in large numbers, too. Some hoverflies have a narrow waist like a wasp, and they'll pretend to sting if you catch them in your hand! The smallest hoverflies grow to be only 0.3 inch (8 mm) long, so they can use all the help they can get against larger predators.

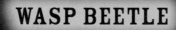

**WASP BEETLE**

## A BEETLE OR A WASP?

The wasp beetle is another harmless invertebrate. It makes up for its small size with its awesome adaptations. These beetles are yellow and black like wasps, and they mimic the flying and walking behaviors of wasps, too. The wasp beetle can also make a buzzing sound to further confuse and scare predators.

HOVERFLIES USE THEIR WASPLIKE FEATURES TO FOOL THE CREATURES THEY MIMIC. THEY SOMETIMES LAY THEIR EGGS IN WASP NESTS. THE LARVAE EAT THE WASPS' LEFTOVER FOOD!

19

One of the best adaptations is the ability to be adaptable. Some animals, such as mice and coyotes, adapt to both warm and cold habitats. The most adaptable creature in the world may be an invertebrate called the tardigrade. These microscopic creatures look a lot like tiny gray bears in space suits. They can survive almost anything!

Tardigrades can live in extreme heat and cold. They can endure great pressure and **radiation**. They can also go very, very long periods without food. **AND IF CONDITIONS FOR LIVING BECOME TOO TOUGH, THEY ENTER A DEATHLIKE STATE FOR YEARS UNTIL THEIR HABITAT IS SUITABLE AGAIN!**

## INVERTEBRATES IN SPACE

Tardigrades have been on Earth for 500 million years. They seem to flourish in any area of Earth. But what about space? In 2007, scientists sent tardigrades into space on a **satellite**. MOST CREATURES WOULD HAVE DIED, BUT TARDIGRADES SURVIVED. Even more amazing, the females laid eggs while in space!

BEFORE ACHIEVING A DEATHLIKE STATE, A TARDIGRADE SUCKS IN ITS HEAD AND EIGHT LEGS, DRIES ITSELF OUT, AND GOES PERFECTLY STILL.

# CRAZY CUCUMBERS

Unlike real cucumbers, sea cucumbers don't look very tasty. These strange, tube-shaped invertebrates live on the ocean floor. They just want to be left alone to eat, but sometimes other creatures bother them.

Sea cucumbers have soft bodies that aren't built for a fight. **HOWEVER, THEY MAKE USE OF AN INCREDIBLE ADAPTATION CALLED EVISCERATION.** That means they shoot parts of their guts out of their body at their attacker! This startles other animals, and sometimes toxins are released as well. Sea cucumbers aren't hurt by evisceration. In fact, they can regrow their lost body parts in only a few weeks.

## CLEAN-UP CREW

Sea cucumbers gather food using tube feet, which look like tentacles around their mouth. They eat detritus, which is ocean waste, and it's a good thing they do. They break down dead animal and plant matter and keep the ocean a cleaner and healthier place for all sea-dwelling creatures.

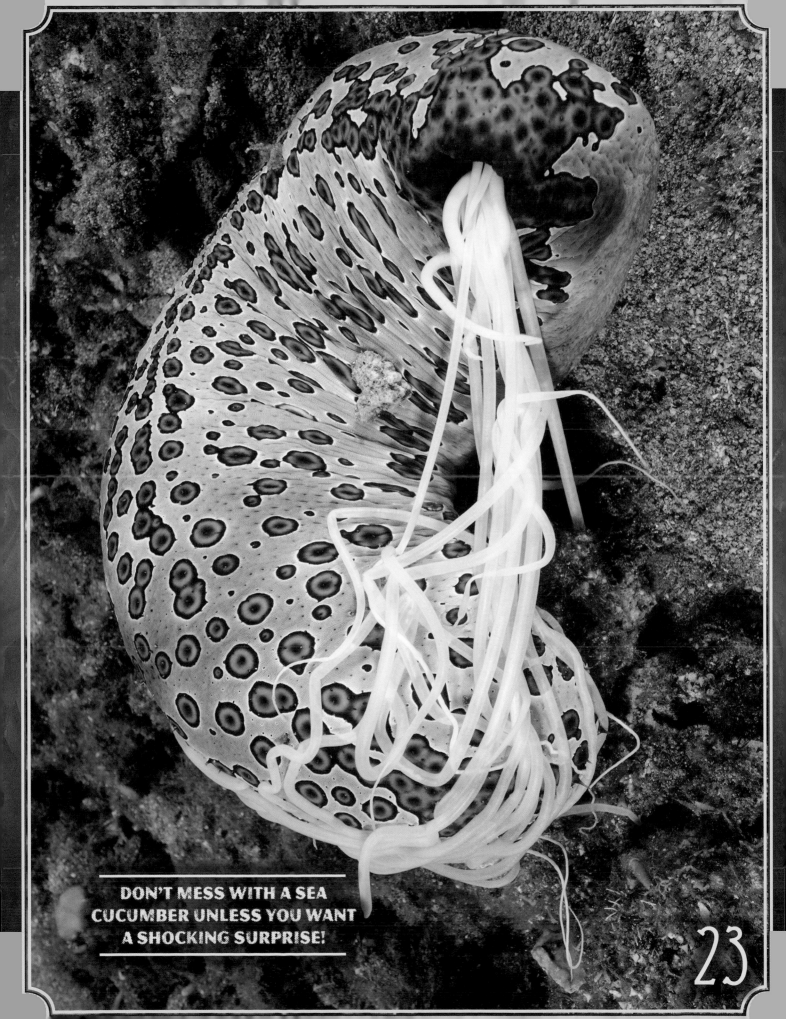

DON'T MESS WITH A SEA
CUCUMBER UNLESS YOU WANT
A SHOCKING SURPRISE!

23

# IT GROWS BACK!

There are about 2,000 species of sea stars, also known as starfish. The five-arm kinds are the most common, but some species have 10, 20, or even 40 arms. Sea stars have an odd adaptation for eating clams or oysters. **WHILE THEIR LEGS HOLD OPEN THE SHELLS, THEIR STOMACH COMES OUT OF THEIR MOUTH TO DIGEST THEIR PREY!**

Sea stars can't run away from attackers, so they may lose an arm or two. However, these invertebrates can regenerate, or regrow, their lost arms. Some species can even grow a whole new body from just part of an arm!

## OTHER ODD ADAPTATIONS

Sea stars move slowly on their 15,000 tiny tube feet. They need all the adaptations they can get against predators. Sea star skin is bony and tough—not exactly an easy-to-eat treat. Some species have skin that camouflages them in their habitat. Other species are bright, to scare away predators.

SCIENTISTS ARE STUDYING
ANIMALS THAT CAN REGENERATE THEIR
LIMBS OR ORGANS. THESE ANIMALS
MIGHT BE THE ANSWER TO HOW
HUMANS CAN DO THE SAME. YOU CAN
SEE A WHOLE NEW BODY GROWING
FROM THIS SEA STAR ARM!

# SMART SPIDERS

Spiders are intelligent invertebrates. **THEY'RE MASTERS OF CAMOUFLAGE AND WEB BUILDING, AND USE VENOM.** More than 40,000 spider species live on Earth, and each one has adapted to its habitat.

Spiders have sharp toothlike fangs to inject venom into their prey, but some spit their venom. All spiders make silk, but not all spiders catch prey with silk webs. Bolas spiders use a sticky blob on the end of a silk line to fish for their food! Some spiders build fake spiders to sit in their web. This is probably to scare off predators, such as wasps. These hunting and defensive adaptations help spiders survive.

**BOLAS SPIDER**

## TRAPDOOR SPIDERS

Trapdoor spiders have an odd behavioral adaptation. They live in little burrows, or holes in the ground, rather than webs. **THEY BUILD TRAPDOORS MADE OF SPIDER SILK, PLANTS, AND SOIL OVER THE BURROW.** Then, they wait under the door for prey to pass by. When it does, the spiders spring into action!

# SPIDER ADAPTATIONS

**STRUCTURAL ADAPTATIONS:**
- VENOM
- CAMOUFLAGE
- WEBS
- EIGHT LEGS
- SENSING LEG HAIRS
- FANGS

**BEHAVIORAL ADAPTATIONS:**
- BUILDING DECOYS
- HUNTING WITH TRAPDOORS
- FISHING FOR PREY
- SPITTING VENOM AT PREY
- BALLOONING (TRAVELING ON A SILK THREAD)

THIS TRAPDOOR SPIDER HIDES IN THE OPENING OF ITS BURROW, WAITING FOR PREY.

# A TOUGH CLAM TO CRACK

The ocean is a tough place to live. Predators are everywhere. What can you do as a soft-bodied, slow creature? In the case of clams, they have a hard shell to keep predators away. They also have a "foot" for digging and hiding themselves.

The largest clam species is the giant clam. **GIANT CLAMS CAN GROW TO BE MORE THAN 4 FEET (1.2 M) LONG AND 400 POUNDS (181 KG).** Once a giant clam finds a place to live, it stays there its whole life—and it can live to be 100. The invertebrate kingdom is full of amazing and odd animals!

## FRIENDLY RELATIONSHIP

Another behavioral adaptation of the giant clam is its relationship with **algae**. Giant clams allow billions of algae to live within them. They get **nutrients** from food made by algae, and the algae get a safe home. This is called a symbiotic relationship. Both animals benefit from it.

PEOPLE ONCE THOUGHT
GIANT CLAMS ATE PEOPLE!
THOSE STORIES HAVE BEEN
DISPROVEN, HOWEVER.

# GLOSSARY

**algae:** simple plantlike things that have no leaves or stems and that grow in or near water

**digest:** to change food into simpler forms that can be used by the body

**habitat:** the place or type of place where a plant or animal naturally or normally lives or grows

**inject:** to use sharp teeth or a stinger to force venom into an animal's body

**microscopic:** something that is invisible without the use of a microscope, a tool for producing a much larger view of small objects

**molt:** to lose a covering and replace it with new growth in the same place

**mutation:** a change in the genes of a plant or animal that causes physical characteristics that are different from what is normal

**nervous system:** the system in the body that carries messages for controlling movement and feeling between body parts

**nutrient:** matter that plants, animals, and people need to live and grow

**paralyze:** to make something lose the ability to move

**radiation:** waves of energy. It can cause health problems in living things exposed to it.

**satellite:** a man-made machine that circles Earth

**tentacle:** a long, thin body part that sticks out from an animal's head or mouth

# FOR MORE INFORMATION

## BOOKS

Marsico, Katie. *Jellyfish*. New York, NY: Children's Press, 2015.

Rice, Dona Herweck. *Traits for Survival*. Huntington Beach, CA: Teacher Created Materials, 2015.

Royston, Angela. *Invertebrates*. Chicago, IL: Capstone Heinemann Library, 2015.

## WEBSITES

**Box Jellyfish**
*www.montereybayaquarium.org/animal-guide/invertebrates/box-jelly*
Learn about the deadly box jellyfish.

**Invertebrates**
*kids.nationalgeographic.com/animals/hubs/invertebrates/*
Check out fun facts about invertebrates.

# INDEX